THE DEFINITIVE GUIDE TO WEDDING FOOD THAT'S LOVED BY Everyone

Dedicated to;

My mum, Lah lah, my very first inspiration in the kitchen.
My wife, Melissa, for her support today and always.
My son, Reni, my newest daily inspiration.

"As cooks, we have the right to heighten and enhance flavours,
we do not have the right to destroy them."
Joel Robuchon

"Food is very much theatre."
James Beard

THE CATERER

*T*hank you for opening this book and having a peek. The recipes in the following pages have been tried and tested and loved by all. This is not a complete guide of what's on offer here at Thomas Towers; it's merely a taster!

My aim is always to create a menu inspired by you and your favourite things; a menu that tells the story of your love and lives together. Whether that's food that makes you reminisce to your travels around the world, a traditional family favourite or a dessert that brings back fond childhood memories; I want to incorporate a little bit of you into your menu.

There are no sample menus, no menu A, B or C, and no silver or gold package with charged optional extras – there is only a menu YOU. Designed by us, created by me, inspired by you.

Whilst the dress, the invites and the décor will all have your personality stamped on it, I believe the food should too!

You might not believe this but this title was the edited version. It could have been a lot longer, but somehow I didn't think that;

"The definitive guide to wedding food that's loved by everyone - but this isn't a comprehensive guide, it's only a taster and in actual fact, you can have entirely what you like from Thomas the Caterer", was particularly catchy. I couldn't see that being a bestseller.

So, get comfortable and turn the page. Let's get started on what I hope will be an inspirational culinary journey. Remember, it's all about you.

Thomas

X

$\mathscr{C}$ongratulations on your engagement!

Whether you're getting married for the first time or re-marrying, you will be embarking on your wedding planning journey, taking the time to consider exactly how you want your day to unfold. Your attention will be drawn to the plethora of wedding ideas and inspiration that exist at the moment – anything from wedding magazines and books to blogs and fabulous (but a little addictive!) online resources like Pinterest.

As a wedding planner, I encourage my clients to keep two important things at the centre of their planning – a) their personality and b) the fact that their wedding day is just the start (albeit an important one) of their married life together – so start as you mean to go on.

Approach your wedding plans with these two things firmly in mind and remember them as you plan each stage and make every decision. Personality and style is often played out in terms of what you choose to wear on the day but it should also influence the type of venue you choose, the way it's decorated, the flowers you select and most certainly, the food you select for your friends and family to enjoy.

Your guests will remember the wonderful wedding location but almost certainly, if the food is bland or lacking creativity, or full of creativity but has no taste, that memory may be more long lasting.

I have worked with clients for whom food has played a significant part in their wedding plans and they have chosen either to reflect places they have visited together in their wedding menu choices or they have simply decided to choose their favourite dishes.

Whether you opt for formal dining or a more relaxed buffet option, the importance of good quality ingredients, great taste and creativity should not be underestimated.

The recipes in this book are a fabulous selection of mouth-watering dishes. Hard for me to select a favourite but I was drawn to the fabulous selection of Antipasti and the delicious and dramatic looking Red Berry Knickerbocker Glory. Use this book either as a guide to help you create some delicious food to wow your guests or to whet your appetite and that of your family and friends in preparation for the quality of food you will be asking your wedding caterers to prepare for you.

Working with Tom over the last couple of years and having sampled his culinary talents I can definitely say that he lives up to his business description of having "generous servings of passion, a bowl full of expertise and a dash of flair". I am happy to recommend Tom to my wedding and event clients because he has a passion for creating food with his clients very much in mind – that and the fact that his pulled pork tortillas with banana and avocado salsa and his chocolate brownies are to die for – Trust me, I've tried them!

Val Mattinson

Wedding Planner and Director
Benessamy Weddings & Events
Midlands Regional Amabassodor for the UK Alliance of Wedding Planners

"On 30th May 2014 Thomas did the catering for our wedding and I can confidently say that he is the King of pie making! Thomas's passion for food, attention to detail and friendly manner is second to none and we can safely say that he produced the best pie and mash we have ever tasted, and it made our day perfect! All our guests keep talking about since our wedding is the quality of Thomas's pies. The father of the bride even said that, if he could, he would put in a weekly order!

Aside from his fantastic culinary skills, what really made Thomas stand apart from the other caterers we met was the way he listened carefully to all our ideas and produced a menu which captured exactly what we wanted and more. He sourced local ingredients, personalised the pies with our initials which was a lovely touch, and spent a lot of time learning how to perfect honeycomb so that he could create the milk chocolate and honeycomb cheesecake dessert the groom had so desired. We would not hesitate to recommend Thomas the Caterer to anyone who is in search of a caterer for their special event and we only hope that we have another occasion to use Thomas's services again in the future.

Thank you Thomas!"

Emma & James

Canapés

ANTIPASTI

**Antipasti boards are a great way to feed the meat eaters and the veggies all in one fell
swoop. Antipasti never lacks flavour and has a continental twist.
It makes for an interesting and stylish canapé option.**

You can really go to town with fancy accompaniments or keep it very simple, opting for a small selection of
quality products from established artisans. Sadly, there is not very much available locally in the East
Midlands, but with antipasti, quality beats quantity every time.

Some examples of great antipasti board fillers are chunky chopped chorizo, wafer thin slices of Parma or
Serrano ham, salami and smoked duck works well and makes an unusual but tasty addition.
On the vegetarian side it goes without saying that olives feature massively with this style of canapé.

Other popular and flavoursome trimmings can include marinated artichokes, pickled vegetables and
mushrooms. Flavoured grissini are fab for the crunch factor.

$\mathscr{L}$ CHICKEN
Liver Parfait

apple puree on toasted brioche

**This is very difficult to make in small batches due to the tender structure of the mixture.
My advice - make a big batch and gorge yourself on parfait. (Or freeze half!)
This would make a great starter too!**

Ingredients – 2 loaf tins • 300g butter • 300g chicken livers • 300g shallots – finely chopped • 200ml brandy • 4 cloves of garlic • 3 eggs • Bunch of thyme • Pink salt or sel rose • Brioche rolls sliced and baked for 5 mins • Your favourite chutney or fruit puree

Place the eggs, butter and livers into separate bowls and leave to get to room temperature. Put shallots in a pan with a dash of oil and sweat down to a lightly coloured mix. Add the brandy, garlic and thyme and reduce until there is very little liquid left in the pan. Leave to cool slightly.

In a large food processor, blend the eggs, butter, livers and shallots mix. Add a generous dash of pink salt (if unavailable table salt will do) and pepper. Pass the mixture through a sieve to remove large pieces. Pour into 2 loaf tins equally. Place the loaf tins in an ovenproof dish. Pour cold water into ovenproof dish and bake for one hour at 115 °C, until the core temperature of the parfait reaches 73°C. Remove from the oven. Chill overnight.

Remove from the fridge the next day and carefully scrape the grey skin off the loaf tin.
Serve with toasted brioche and chutney. Delicious!

ROCKET

A fairly recent discovery for me. Worth keeping in your repertoire as all your guests will love it and they taste great!

Ingredients (makes 18-20) - 25g butter • 25g flour • 125g whole milk • 50g cheddar cheese • Salt and pepper • 150g roasted silverside of beef chopped very small • 150g button mushrooms chopped and sautéed • A splash of dark soy sauce
To crumb - 2 eggs • 200g plain flour • 200g breadcrumbs

Melt the butter and flour in a large pan, stirring constantly until you have a mixture that looks like wet sand. Add the milk and continue to cook until thick and smooth. Add the cheese, season well and stir in. Remove from the heat and allow to cool. Add the beef and the mushrooms to the cheese sauce along with a good splash of soy sauce. Mix well, taste test and season if necessary.

Put this mixture into a piping bag and pipe rows onto baking parchment. Freeze until solid and then chop up into small sausage sizes.

To crumb the Krocket, roll the sausage shapes in flour, shake off any excess and dip into the beaten egg, then into the bread crumbs so its completely covered in crumbs. If it's not, dab into the egg again, then back into the crumbs. Leave them to these defrost in the fridge then deep fry at 180°C for about 3 minutes. Serve with mustard or ketchup! Delicious!

PEA & TRUFFLE
Oil Soup Shots

Little tip - I like to serve this in shot glasses using a jug or tea pot! Add a few drips of truffle oil on the top and hey presto!

Ingredients (Serves 6 or 18 shot glasses) – Small bag of peas 500g • A knob of unsalted butter • 500ml of vegetable stock • 1 onion – finely chopped • 3 cloves of garlic – finely chopped • Salt and pepper • A few drops of truffle oil.

Gently melt the butter in a large pan before adding the onion and garlic. Sauté until translucent, add the stock and bring to the boil. Once boiling, add the frozen peas (uncooked) and remove from the heat. Season with salt and pepper and blend well using a food processor or stick blender.

Pass this mixture through a fine sieve to remove any large bits not blended in the pureeing process. Serve as you wish.

VIETNAMESE EM

Oh wow - These are the bestest! I'm very jealous that Vietnamese people can enjoy these so regularly!

Ingredients (Serves 6 or one greedy chef!) - A pack of Vietnamese rice paper circles - 22cm • 200g pork mince • 200g bean sprouts • The zest and juice of 1 lime • 1 red chilli chopped and deseeded • Half a red and yellow pepper, sliced • 1 tbsp of sugar • Small bunch of coriander

Fry off the pork in a dry frying pan until all the moisture evaporates and the meat becomes crispy. Try to get loads of colour in it (remember colour = flavour)

Leave to cool in a bowl. Once cooled, add the chilli, the zest, peppers and juice of one lime, the sugar, the coriander and the bean sprouts. Taste this mix, add salt if necessary.

When the mixture is prepared, follow the instructions found on the rice paper packet. Normally I work with one paper soaking whilst working on one it makes the process go quicker. It's fiddly to begin with but stick with it – it will be more than worth it!

Serve with some soy sauce or sweet chilli dipping sauce.

Enjoy!

YORKSHIRE PUDDING,
BRAISED BEEF
& HORSERADISH SAUCE

Top Tip - Make your batter the day before so the flour has time to break down and rest. Using a mini Yorkshire pudding tray is the key to getting perfect tiny puds.

Ingredients (makes 24 miniature Yorkshire Puddings) - 4 eggs • 200ml whole milk • 140g plain flour salt and pepper • Sunflower oil for the tray • 500g - diced chuck steak (make sure you have at least 27 pieces a couple for tasting!) • 1 tbsp plain flour • 1 litre of water • Bay leaf • 3 garlic cloves crushed • 1 onion diced 1 carrot diced • 1 beef stock cube • 1/5 fresh horseradish • 3 tbsp mayonnaise

Crack the eggs into a bowl, add the milk and slowly add the flour to make a batter add the salt and pepper quite heartily. Ideally, mixture should be left to rest overnight. Minimum resting time should be no less than two hours.

In a bowl cover the beef in the plain flour then seal the beef in a frying pan, then place in a high sided pan, cover with the water and stock cube and bring to the boil. Add the onion, carrot, bay leaf and garlic and cook until tender. This will take at least an hour and a half.

When the beef is nearly cooked, place your yorkie tin in the oven (without any oil in) at 230 °C. Leave it to warm up for ten minutes before adding a good dash of oil in each pudding hole. Return it to the oven until the oil is smoking hot.

Very carefully remove the tray from the oven again (it will be dangerously hot!) Pour the batter from a jug into the moulds. It should make a hissy cracking noise - this is great news! Return the tray to the oven and watch those babies grow!

Whilst the yorkies are cooking get your goggles out! Peel the horseradish and using the finest grater you have to grate the remaining root. Try not to cry - this stings more than onions! Add this mixture to the mayonnaise and season well with salt and pepper.

Place the cooked, tender pieces of beef in the cooked Yorkshire Puds and a dib of sauce.

DOLCETATTE FIG BRUSCETTAS
fine herbs & balsamic dressing

A really flavoursome canapé.

1 x 6" Ciabatta • 125 g dolcelatte • Pack of dried figs or fresh if available • Small bunch of dill, parsley, basil and chives - chopped finely • Reduced balsamic syrup (easily bought from the super market)

Cut the ciabatta down the middle lengthways, then slice thinly (about 0.5 cm). Lay them on a tray and bake in the oven, until slightly golden. Remove from the oven and cool.

In a bowl place three or four dried figs and pour on a little boiling water to rehydrate slightly. Break the cheese up and push it gently onto the bruschetta's. Chop the figs into pieces of either 6 or 8, depending on size. Place on top of the cheese. Drizzle with balsamic glaze and sprinkle with herbs.

"We were looking for a caterer for our wedding, and came across Thomas's website. We exchanged emails, and it became apparent immediately that his focus was on creating a menu that suited our wants, not what was easiest for him to make. He came to see us, and we were both very impressed with the thought and effort that he had put in to the presentation he gave us, creating the bones of what would go on to be the basis of our wedding breakfast.

Thomas was enthusiastic about the elements of food that we were looking to incorporate in our menu, namely regionalism and seasonality, and produced an excellent menu, full of local specialties. He was very attentive throughout the process, checking that his ideas were hitting the mark, and making sure that everything was ready for the wedding, including cutlery and glasses etc. He was also very personable. It was also very original in its presentation, with the idea of picnic boxes and guests serving themselves, and the clever way that the chocolate mousse suggested a field with a sprig of mint growing out of it.

On the day itself, Thomas and his team were very hard working and enthusiastic, looking to make the day go as smoothly as possible. They were very friendly and approachable, as well as being very smartly turned out. The food itself was wonderful and beautifully presented. All of our guests commented on the presentation style, the deliciousness of the food and the originality of the concept, with many commenting that it was the best wedding food that they'd ever had.

Thomas's food and his team went a long way to making our day so memorable. It was if a friend was preparing the food for us, rather than a catering company. My husband and I, and I'm sure anyone who tasted his food on the day, would not hesitate in recommending him for any event. Indeed, the next time that we have any sort of event he will be the first person that we call."

Thomas & Lauren Kivits-Murray

STARTERS

$\mathcal{G}$OATS CHEESE
RED ONION TART

Ingredients (serves 8) - 1 pack of ready rolled puff pastry • 500g red onions – finely sliced • 100ml red wine • 100ml white wine vinegar • 100g brown sugar • 250g goat's cheese

Put onions in a pan with enough oil to grease the pan slightly. Sweat them down as though you're making onions for hot dogs. When the onions are soft and slightly translucent add the red wine and the white wine vinegar - begin to reduce. Stir frequently. When the liquid is reduced by approximately half, add the sugar and continue to reduce until there is little or no liquid left.

At this point you can remove from the heat and place in a clean sterile container. This marmalade mixture will keep for 6 weeks in the fridge. Pre heat the oven to 190 °C.

Unroll the pastry and cut into 15cm x 6cm rectangles. Place on a lined baking tray. Cover with a sheet of baking parchment and place another baking tray on top of it. This will stop the puff pastry puffing too much and will make it really crispy.

Bake for 15 minutes or until the pastry is crispy and golden brown. Remove from the oven and place two or three dessert spoons of the onion marmalade on top of the pastry. Crumble or slice your goat's cheese top of the onions (it will depend on how mature it is). Return to the oven for approximately 5 minutes, or until the cheese begins to brown slightly.

Serve with dressed salad leaves and vinaigrette.

SALMON CRAB
AND CORIANDER
TIMBALE

Ingredients (serves 6) – 250g salmon fillet • 200g salt • 200g sugar • 5 limes • 200g fresh crab claw meat
• Bunch of coriander • 100ml crème fraiche • 1/3 cucumber - sliced thinly
• 1/3 cucumber diced small

Two days before serving this dish, zest and juice three limes and add the mixture to the salt and the sugar.
Put the salmon in a bowl; cover with this mix and leave to cure.

After 2 days, remove the fish from the mixture – rinse and pat dry before chopping
into small dice.

In a new bowl add the crab, salmon, the coriander, the crème fraiche and diced cucumber. Mix well and taste
- it won't need any more salt but you will need more lime juice and zest to lift the flavour.

Now comes the impressive cheffy part! Using ring moulds or ramekins, line the rings with sliced cucumber
around the interior. Place the salmon and crab mix into the rings. Remove the ring leaving a fancy looking
(and perfectly spherical) "crown". Surround this with light soft herby salad
leaves and serve.

$\mathscr{S}$ TOMATO AND BASIL
OUP TAPENADE POTATOES

Ingredients (serves 6) - 12 plum tomatoes • 1 banana shallot • 2 cloves of garlic • Sprig of thyme
200 ml vegetable stock • 1 tin of chopped tomatoes • Large bunch of fresh basil • 200g new
potatoes cooked and peeled

Tapenade - 50g pitted black olives • 2 anchovies • 20g capers

Begin by sweating the shallots in a little oil, add the garlic and thyme and continue to cook gently. Add the
fresh and tinned tomatoes and turn the heat up. Next, add the stock and simmer gently for 15 minutes.
Remove from the heat and leave to cool slightly. Add the fresh basil and use a stick blender to puree the soup
until smooth. Pass this through a sieve to remove any large bits.

To make the tapenade, add all the ingredients to a small blender and mix into a coarse paste.
Mix the tapenade with the cooked potatoes and place a pile in each of the soup bowls.
Create a little food theatre and pour the soup over the potatoes in front of your guests. Use a lovely jug or
teapot for maximum effect.

Wild
MUSHROOM
Aranchini

Ingredients (makes 36) - 200g Arborio risotto rice • 1.5l vegetable stock • Large glass white wine • 1 large Spanish onion – chopped finely • 5 cloves of garlic • 400g mixed wild mushrooms • Small bunch of flat leaf parsley • 125g dried wild mushrooms • 100g Parmesan • 250g panko bread crumbs (not very Italiano but the best bread crumbs around!) • 3 eggs • 150 g plain flour

Make up the stock with boiled water and add in the dried mushrooms to rehydrate. Fry off the onion in a large pan with a little olive oil.

Add the Arborio rice and get some heat into it before adding the glass of white wine. From this point on, the mixture needs constant stirring. Remove the mushrooms from the stock and set aside.

Let the rice almost completely soak up the wine before adding the stock 50ml by 50ml. Let the rice soak up the liquid before adding the next measure. Stir constantly (your arm will ache but it's worth it!)
When the stock is nearly all used up add the garlic and have a little taste test to ensure it's all cooked through. If it needs more liquid – add in a little more, but be sparing.

Chop up the fresh mushrooms and fry them off in a large pan, getting good all over colour. Add these to the risotto mix. Roughly chop the dried mushrooms and parsley and add this alongside the grated Parmesan to the risotto mix. Stir well and remove from the heat. Let the mix cool. Taste and season accordingly.

Next, line a tray with baking parchment and roll the risotto into balls about the size of a ping-pong ball. Let the balls chill in the fridge. A great tip is to freeze them – this makes them easier to handle for the next step.

Using three large bowls – one with the panko breadcrumbs, one with the beaten egg and one with flour. Take one ball and roll evenly in the flour. Then dip it in the egg mix, cover completely, drain slightly and then roll in panko breadcrumbs. You should now be left with one risotto ball covered in bread crumbs.

Well done! Now repeat!

You can bake these but deep frying gets the best results. Deep fry the Arancini for 4 minutes until golden brown. Serve with freshly grated Parmesan and rocket or alternatively, as a side dish to grilled meats and veggies.

TRADITIONALLY
DRESSED
Smoked Salmon

Ingredients (serves 6) – 300g smoked salmon • 2 tbsp capers • 1 banana shallot • 1 lemon
Black pepper • Brown bread and butter

Chop the shallots as finely as you can. Lay the salmon on the plate in one layer -sprinkle over some shallots
and capers, grind pepper over it and a squeeze of lemon.

Serve with fresh brown bread and butter with the crusts cut off.

Cured BEEF
fennel, radish chilli and Lime salad

Ingredients (serves 8) – 250g sugar • 250g salt • 3 juniper berries crushed • 2 bay leaves • 3 cloves of garlic • The zest and juice of one lime • 500g piece of trimmed top side beef (no fatty bits or sinews)

Salad - 200g radish • 1 red chilli diced very small • 1 lime • 1 bulb of fennel

Mix all the ingredients (except the beef) in a large bowl. Make a parting in the middle of the mixture and place the beef in it. Put the mixture over the beef, cover with cling film and leave in the fridge for one week.

Slice the radish and fennel as finely as possible. Dice the chilli into tiny cubes. Remove the beef from the salty sugary mixture and rinse under cold water - discard the remaining liquid.

Pat the beef dry and place on a chopping board. Slice off wafer thin slices and lay it directly onto a plate. I think this is served beautifully as a sharing platter so opt for a large plate. Scatter the radish and fennel slices over the beef then sprinkle on the chilli and the zest the lime. Next, squeeze the juice over and drizzle some olive oil across the plate.

Voila! A taste sensation!

BREAKFAST SALAD

Essentially this is a mega starter for the guys. I hope that they will have had a big brekkie before walking down the aisle but just in case, this starter is always a winner!

Imagine all your favourite breakfast items served on a delicious dressed salad, topped with a poached egg - what's not to like?!

Quite simply make this as though you were going to make a fry up grilling and frying all your fave ingredients (bacon/pancetta, sausages, sautéed potatoes, tomatoes, mushrooms – whatever you fancy).

Chop it all up, leave to cool a little and served on some lovely crunchy salad. Top tip – opt for a sharp vinaigrette dressing. It will cut through the delicious fat in the sausages and give tons of flavour!

BALLONTINE OF CHICKEN
& sun blushed tomatoes *with*
olives & dressed leaves

Ingredients (serves 8) - 2 chicken breasts • 200g sun blushed tomatoes • Large bunch of basil

Lay a few layers of cling film out on your desk. Turn the chicken breast on its back and "butterfly" it open to make one very flat, thin piece of chicken. Repeat with the other breast then lay them, slightly overlapping, onto the cling film (should be approximately 20 cm long). Season well with salt and pepper.

Lay the basil leaves down the length of the chicken so you have a green stripe about 8 cm wide along the whole length of the chicken. Now add the tomatoes evenly down the middle of the chicken.

Now, very carefully, roll the chicken up to make a large "sausage" folding the cling film into the sausage to seal everything in. Tie the ends up with a knot to make a tight sausage. (You may need help with this – it can be a little tricky.) Now poach in water, in a wide shallow pan for about an hour or until a temperature probe reads 75 °C. Place on a tray and chill in the fridge - ideally overnight.

To make the dressing, squeeze the juice of one lemon into a bowl with a generous glug of olive oil, 50g of chopped mixed olives and some finely chopped chives.

To serve, cut a slice from the sausage and place it on the plate, surrounded with salad leaves. Spoon on the olive dressing.

JESSICA&AARON

a ROCK N ROLL WEDDING

"We couldn't have dreamed of a better menu than the one Thomas created for us. The food was absolutely amazing and exactly how we had imagined it. Everything from the day we met Thomas to our wedding day was flawless, fun and funky!

Not only was the food awesome, he is the nicest guy you will ever work with and nothing was too much trouble for him to do for our day. He went from Thomas the caterer to Thomas our Friend."

Forever Grateful

Aaron & Jess

Mains

CHICKEN SUPREME

TARRAGON FONDANT POTATO
creamed
Savoy cabbage
and roasted carrots

Ingredients (serves 4) - 4 Chicken Supremes – (Chicken breast, skin on, wing bone in tact) • 4 large potatoes - peeled (Maris piper are best) • ½ savoy cabbage • 4 large carrots - peeled • 200ml double cream • 250g unsalted butter • Bulb of garlic • Thyme • Salt and pepper • 100ml chicken stock

Cut your peeled potatoes into thick ice hockey puck sized discs. Crush the bulb of garlic, bruise the thyme and pop all of this into a cold oven proof, non-stick pan. Chop the butter into cubes and dot it around the potatoes. Put it on the heat, add the stock and bring to the boil.

Once boiling put the pan in the oven at 200 °C for about 30-45 minutes the stock will evaporate and the butter will caramelize the bottom of the potatoes. Place your peeled carrots in a large roasting tin and drizzle with oil. Bake them for around 35-45 minutes until tender.

To cook the chicken supremes in a pan with a little oil on the hob. Transfer to a tray to finish cooking for 25 minutes until the flesh feels firm to touch. If you have temperature probe the core temperature shoud reach 75 degrees.

Shred the cabbage and blanch in salted, boiling water. Drain and cool under running water. Squeeze out all of the excess water and set aside. Put the cream in a pan and reduce by half, seasoning with a little salt and pepper. Add the cabbage to the cream and bring to the boil stirring frequently. Remove the chicken from the oven and rest.

Serve – I like to put the potato on plates first, with the cabbage on top, then the chicken and carrots. This gives the dish some height and will make it look as appetising as it tastes!

THE
Ultimate
BURGER!

You can get the whole family involved in making these bad boys!

Ingredients (serves 6) - 1.5kg fresh ground mince beef • 1 large red onion - finely diced
• 1tsp dried Italian herbs • 1tsp mustard

Brioche Buns - 300g strong flour • 36g castor sugar • 6g salt • 150g butter • 12g fresh yeast
20ml water • 3 eggs

Blend the flour, sugar, salt and butter in a mixer – it should turn into a mixture that resembles breadcrumbs.
Mix the yeast and water together and add to mixture before adding the beaten eggs.

This will make a wet mixture. Work it well and turn into a large bowl and leave it in the fridge overnight. The next day, split the dough into 6 evenly sized balls using the palms of your hands. Roll them out into balls and leave at room temperature on a lined baking tray until they have doubled in size – (this should take approximately 3 hours).

Use a beaten egg to lightly glaze the buns just before going into the oven to bake at 180 °C for 15-20 minutes.

Mix the beef, dried herbs, mustard and seasoning in a bowl. Split the mixture into 6 evenly sized meat patties and rest in the fridge. Ultimately you should cook these on the BBQ but a grill will do if it's raining! Remember the flavour is in the colour so get them nice and brown! They should need around 15-20 minutes under a hot grill turning half way through.

FILLET OF BEEF

$\mathcal{P}$OTATO ROSTI
green beans, roasted baby onions

$\mathcal{O}$NION PUREE

Ingredients (serves 4) - 4 x 200g beef fillets • 3 large Maris Piper potatoes - peeled • 400g green beans • 20 baby onions or shallots • 2 large Spanish onions • A few knobs of butter • 100ml double cream

Grate the peeled potatoes and season very well with salt (this will draw out the liquid from the spud). Place the grated potato onto a clean tea towel and squeeze out all the remaining water.

Heat a large pan, adding a good glug of oil. Make 4 piles of grated potato pushing down with a spatula to make 4 'pancakes'. Lower the heat and gently move around the pan until you're confident they won't break if moved. Turn the rosti over and continue to cook on this side adding a little butter as you go. Add the shallots or baby onions and this point and continue cooking in the oven until the potatoes are looking lovely and crisp!

For the puree, chop your onions the smallest you can and sweat them in a little butter until translucent. Add the cream, season well and reduce by half. Put this mixture in a food processor and puree, then push it through a sieve to ensure it's nice and smooth.

In salted boiling water, cook the green beans until they're tender (approximately 3-4 minutes) - drain and toss in a little butter.

Cook the beef to your liking either on a griddle pan or in a frying pan. I would air on the side of caution and under cook rather than over cook! It is fillet after all! Make the presentation fun! Perhaps copy how I have served it or make it up!

Rump of

LAMB

Aubergine purée,

RATATOUILLE,
AND *Sauté* POTATOES

Ingredients (serves 4) – 2 Lamb rumps • 500g new potatoes • 2 aubergines • 1 red pepper
1 green pepper • 1 yellow pepper • 1 courgette • 100ml double cream

Pre-heat the oven and place the aubergine on a tray, whole, drizzled with oil. Cover it with foil and forget
about it in the oven for a whole hour.

Put the new potatoes in cold water; bring them to the boil and cook gently until tender.
Now it's time to get your chop on! Dice all the remaining veggies as small as you possibly can. Heat a splash
of olive oil in a frying pan, and begin to sauté the veggies in batches, the peppers then all the courgette
(they all have different cooking times). Then mix the cooked veggies together and voila! A simple ratatouille.
Season this to taste.

When the potatoes are cooked remove from the heat, drain well and run under cold water to cool slightly.
Cut them in half and put your deep fat fryer on to 190 °C.

Remove the aubergine from the oven, chop it up into smaller pieces and place into a jug before adding the
cream to it. Blend to a puree and season well. Now pass this through a sieve to ensure the mixture is smooth.

Seal off the lamb in a hot pan then roast in the oven for 15 minutes or until browned all over. Rest for 5
minutes. In this time, fry the potatoes until they are golden brown. Carve the meat up and arrange the
veggies around it beautifully!

PORK FILLET
Chorizo,
LITTLE GEM LETTUCE, PEAS
and baby potaotes

Ingredients (serves 4) - 1 whole pork fillet • 100g of sliced chorizo • 4 baby gem lettuces • 400g peas • 500g new potatoes • 200ml cream • ¼ chicken stock cube • 1 small glass of white wine

Trim the pork of any sinews or white fatty bits, then cut into 4 equal sized loins (you could ask your butcher to do this for you).

Using a sharp knife to cut into the meat on the longest side. Cut through the meat but not entirely to the other side - keep it one piece. Repeat this again so by the end you have one flat piece of pork - it should be rectangular. Repeat for all the pork then lay the chorizo in a layer over the pork. Roll up like a roulade and wrap in cling film like a Ballontine (see Chicken Ballontine). Secure each end by knotting the cling film before poaching in hot water for 30 minutes.

Cook the new potatoes as normal and once cooked, cut in half.

For the fricassee of peas and baby gem; cut each of the lettuce into 4 leaving the stork intact so the leaves don't fall apart. In a large skillet or frying pan, reduce the wine and chicken stock slightly before adding the cream, potatoes and peas. At the very end, add the lettuce and cook for two minutes (the lettuce wants to be hot but not too wilted).

Place this mixture in 4 bowls. Remove the pork from the water and get rid of the cling film. Slice each piece into 4 and lay on top of the little gem lettuce.

Sausage
AND
MASH

Buy THE best sausages you find. Getting cheap, rusk heavy, sausages will be flavourless and are no good. Get a butcher to make sausage for you - you won't regret it!

Ingredients (serves 4) - 8 sausages (I prefer Lincolnshire but pork are good too) • 8 large potatoes (Maris Piper or King Edwards are good) • 100g butter • 100ml double cream • Dash of Nutmeg • Salt and freshly ground pepper • 2 red onions - peeled and cut into wedges • 500ml beef stock • 50g flour • 50g butter

Peel the potatoes and cut into small, evenly sized pieces. Put in a pan with a generous teaspoonful of salt and cover with cold water. Place on the heat and cook until soft.

At the same time place the sausages and onion wedges in a tray and roast for 25-30 minutes in the oven at 200 °C.

Boil the beef stock in a large pan.
Massage the butter and flour together to make a cement like mixture - whisk this into the stock to make the gravy. This will make it just right consistency. You can add more flavour by adding herbs such as rosemary, thyme and garlic. Adding a little red wine or beer right at the end also works well for a strong flavour hit! (Alternatively, you can use readymade granules - I do sometimes)

When the potatoes are cooked, drain well and leave to dry. Return to the pan and mash well, adding the butter, the cream, salt, pepper and a little nutmeg.
Once the sausages are cooked and the onions have caramelised, you're ready to plate up! Whack a generous serving of mash in a bowl, top with the sausages and onions and cover with gravy!

FISH AND CHIPS

Ingredients (serves 4) - 1 Pint of ale • 4 cod, haddock or hake fillets (around 200-300g pieces) • 4 large potatoes (Maris piper ideally) 500g Plain flour • Salt • A large pinch of Baking Powder • 400g frozen peas.

I know what you're thinking, FROZEN PEAS? A chef and frozen PEAS?? I have to say they are brilliant and really user friendly, taste great and are darn handy! I always have peas in my freezer!

Begin with the batter – it's always better when it's rested slightly. Pour the ale into a large bowl, add a good helping of salt and a tea spoon of baking powder. Gradually whisk in the flour until the mixture is thicker than a pancake batter but thinner than custard! Leave this to rest whist you make the other bits…

Chop your peeled potatoes into thick or thin chips (whichever you prefer). Try and get them all roughly the same size. Blanch in your fryer at 130 °C, until soft and looking like yummy chip shop chips. Remove from the fryer, drain well and set aside. Turn the fryer up to 190 °C.

Cook your peas in a pan of boiling water, drain well and put them in your food processor with a knob of butter and a little salt and pepper to taste.

You may have asked your fish monger to skin your fish. If not, skin it! Sprinkle the fish with flour, shake off any excess and dip into your lovely rested batter. Carefully place into the hot oil. You will need to flip the fish occasionally using a set of kitchen tongs.

When the fish is nearly done (should be approximately 12 minutes), add the chips back into the fryer. You may find that you need to do this in batches.

Serve with a good wedge of fresh lemon and some tartar sauce if you like it! Oh don't forget the bread and butter! For me, it has to be white bread!

STEAK & BELVOIR BEER PIE

tonnes of Veggies *&* Gravy

A great British classic. Perfect when shared amongst family and friends.

Ingredients (Serves 4 greedy cooks) - 1 large onion – diced finely • 2 cloves of garlic - crushed • 1kg beef chuck steak - diced • 500ml beef stock • 2tbsp plain flour • 1 pint of Belvoir ale • Bay Leaf • 1 egg to egg wash

Pastry - 400g plain flour • 250g butter • 1 egg • 2tbsp water • Salt

In a large bowl, rub in the butter, salt and flour together between your fingers. You should aim to get a mixture with a similar consistency to bread crumbs. Beat the egg and water together then add it to the flour mixture. Knead it together then leave it to rest for one hour minimum. This prevents the pastry contracting in the oven.

Heat a tbsp of oil in a large pan. Add the onions, garlic and the beef to the pan, seasoning well. When it all has a great brown colour to it, sprinkle over the flour and mix well then add the stock, the bay leaf and half the ale and leave to simmer.

Stir frequently until the meat is tender. You can only check this by doing a taste test! Let the meat cool slightly whilst you roll out the pastry.

Split the pastry into thirds reserving one third for the lid. Roll out your pastry to half a centimetre thickness to line the bottom of your pie dish.

Stir in the remaining ale (this will give a really ale-y flavour to your pie), and spoon the filling into the pie dish. Roll out the lid to roughly the same shape as the pie dish, beat the egg and using a brush, paint the edges of the pastry. Lay the lid on top of this and crimp using a fork or spoon handle. Cut the spare pastry away from the edges and brush well with the remaining egg wash. Make two holes with a skewer to let the steam out in the lid.

Bake in the oven at 200 °C for about 30-45 minutes. Share and enjoy!

HAUNCH of *Venison*,
WILD MUSHROOMS, SWEDE, KALE
& château potatoes

Okay, so Chateau Potatoes are just a 'cheffy' name for roast potatoes. If you want authentic Chateau Potatoes, YouTube them, but the method I'm going to tell you is almost identical and just as tasty!

Ingredients (Serves 4) - 800g Venison Haunch - cut into 4 steaks • 1tbsp plain flour • Glass of red wine • 1 litre beef stock • 400g wild mushrooms (any variety – whatever's in season) • ½ swede - peeled and chopped • 500g kale • 4 large baking potatoes – peeled • 125g butter

Roll the steaks in flour sealing in all the flavour. Seal the venison off in a hot pan with a little oil. Throw a little butter into the pan once it's nicely coloured. Add the wine to this to deglaze the pan then cover with stock and simmer gently until tender – this should take approximately 1.5 to 2 hours.

Now onto the Chateau Potatoes! Cut your peeled potatoes into evenly sized pieces and pop them into a large pan of cold salted water. Put them on the heat and bring to the boil – then drain and leave them to dry off. Meanwhile... Get a large frying pan that is oven safe. Pop on the hob with a little sunflower or vegetable oil and let it heat up. Once the oil is hot, add the potatoes and colour well all over, seasoning well with salt and pepper. Add 125g of butter and let it melt amongst the potatoes. It will begin to foam but don't panic! This is BEAUTIFUL - And exactly what you want! Add in a small bunch of thyme and half a bulb of crushed garlic. Place them in the oven (in the same pan) at 180 °C for 30-35 minutes until soft and fluffy in the centre. Now get the swede on, boil this from cold water with a good amount to salt. Once tender, drain well then return to the pan to crush with a masher. Add generous amounts of pepper.

The kale needs only a few seconds in boiling water so be very careful not to overcook it. My grandma used to say that bad hospitality is when you get kale cooked twice! YUCK!

Sauté off the wild mushrooms in a frying pan. Start by lightly cooking the big ones first then adding the smaller ones in later. Serve as desired!

Picnic
THEME

You may love stilton, roasted beef and scotch eggs. I know "I Do" (jokes).

You might know a local baker who makes the most amazing sour dough bread that you want to include alongside some homemade specialities like chutneys, pate, and rustic salads made with seasonal veggies. Decide on your own combinations of the freshest seasonal produce, delicious local cheese and meat and all the scrumptious added extras, all served up in hampers or apple boxes or any other way you wish!

The picnic options pictured includes;
Roasted Local Meats
Potted Shrimps
Freshly Baked Breads
Fresh Fruit
Mixed Salads, Coleslaw, Hummus
Pork Pie
Scotch Eggs
Stilton
(Other cheeses are available too,
but "I do" love stilton)

Afternoon Tea Party

What could be more quintessentially romantic than sitting in your amazing wedding dress, having a quaint cup of tea served from pretty china teacups?

With an Afternoon Tea style wedding breakfast, you can choose which delectable treats you want to include. Whilst my favourite sandwich is peanut butter and cucumber, I don't feel the need to enforce this in all the Afternoon Tea's I create! You may wish to stick to traditional smoked salmon and cream cheese sandwiches with scones and Victoria Sponge, or you might want something more individual and personal to you.

Here is a sample menu for some Afternoon Tea style Wedding Catering I did this summer…

Cut Sandwiches
Cream Cheese and Cucumber
Jubilee Chicken
Cheese and Tomato Chutney
Smoked Salmon and Herb Mascarpone
Ham and Mustard Mayonnaise

Then…
Chorizo and Apple Sausage Rolls
Goats Cheese, Red Onion and Cherry Tomato Tart
Quails Eggs and Black Pudding Scotch Eggs

Followed by…
Scones with Clotted Cream and Jam,
Lemon Drizzle Cake,
Thomas the Caterer's Famous Chocolate Brownies
Raspberry Meringue Kisses

ℒROCK N ROLLERS
OADS OF DIFFERENT DISHES

I call it Rock n Roll because it breaks all the rules!

There isn't any formality with this style of service. Imagine
3, 4 or even 5 of your favourites dishes served in miniature.
Sort of similar to tapas but with anything you like!

Pictured for an example are;

Lamb and Chorizo Ragu with Pesto and Ciabatta Crisps
Mini Burgers
Thai Green Chicken Curry
Chilli Con Carne, Lime Salsa and Nachos

I know it's not really Rock n Roll but I like it!

"Originally I had an alternative caterer booked who let me down 5 months to the wedding so I was very apprehensive about finding and trusting another caterer, then along came Thomas.

From the moment I met Thomas he made me feel at ease, he was professional yet caring. I was totally up front with Thomas and said while food is your passion for me its a necessity for the wedding and while I'd like it to be beautiful in taste and appearance, I do have a budget to stick to.

Thomas listened carefully and advised tastefully on options within our budget, to me this was perfect as so many caterers fit you and your wedding around the menu but Thomas fits the menu around your wedding. He made me realise that my thought process around the food being a 'necessity' was actually not true it was such a huge part of the day. 7 months on and our guests still tell us how amazing the food was and how it perfectly portrayed our style for food.

On the days leading up to the wedding Thomas was a god send, I don't know what I would have done without him. His calming and positive attitude enabled me to relax and know that it was all going to be fine.

On the day itself Thomas and his team were fantastic, as soon as Ian and I arrived back from the church as husband and wife Thomas was there to greet us with his huge infectious smile.

The service was faultless and their ability to work around us was just perfect as our guests decided to party for hours which meant Thomas was a lot
later leaving the venue than planned but not once did he complain.

Thank you to Thomas and his team for making our day so perfect."

Lauren Hulme

DESSERTS

Mr & Mrs

Love heart
MERINGUES

The most romantic dessert ever?!

Ingredients (serves 8) – 150g egg whites • 300g-castor sugar • 300g mixed red berries • 1 vanilla pod • 100ml water • 100g-castor sugar • 300ml double cream

Pre heat the oven to 180 °C. Spread the sugar on a sheet of baking parchment on a tray and put it in the oven. Whisk the egg whites slowly using a stand alone mixer.

Keep an eye on the sugar - you want the edges to just begin to melt. Increase the speed on the whites and begin to shake the sugar onto the mixture slowly. This will "cook" the whites and will help create a more stable meringue mixture. Turn the oven down to 100 °C.

Beat well until glossy, well risen and slightly cooled. Place this mixture into a piping bag and line two large trays with baking parchment. Snip the end off the piping bag, make a 1cm hole and pipe heart shapes and little nests using even amounts of mixture for both shapes. Place in the oven and bake for around 1 hour, or until you can lift the meringues off the tray without them breaking.

Whip the cream in a large bowl with the seeds scraped from the vanilla pod, add the sugar gradually, whisking until the cream gets soft peaks. Cover and leave in the fridge until serving.
Heat 100ml of water on a low heat, in a small pan with the vanilla pod and sugar. Bring to the boil and reduce by half. Then leave to cool.

Prepare the red fruits as normal - discard and greenery or bruised bits.
Place the baked meringues onto a plate add a dollop of cream and spoonful of berries, drizzle with syrup and add the heart shaped meringue on top.

Enjoy!

CHOCOLATE CHEESECAKE

Ingredients (serves 12 - makes one large cake) - 230g ginger nuts • 100g butter melted • 600g cream cheese
500ml cream • 4 eggs • 170g castor sugar • 300g dark chocolate
Top tip – make sure all your ingredients are at room temperature before you start.

Melt the butter and blitz the biscuits into a powder. Combine the two together then press evenly into the
bottom of a lined cake tin.

Melt the chocolate in a pan with a dash of the cream. In a separate bowl, beat together the remaining ingredients well. Once the chocolate has melted, add it to your bowl of wet ingredients and blend together. Pour into
the tin and bake at 180°C for one hour.
When the cheese cake has been in the oven for an hour or the centre has just a little wobble, remove from the
oven. Chill overnight or a minimum of 4 hours to let it cool off completely serve this with fresh red berries
and pouring cream.

STICKY TOFFEE PUDDING

Every Dad's favourite!

Ingredients (serves 8) - 270g dates - chopped • 415ml water • 1 vanilla pod - split and seeds scraped out • 1.5 tsp bi-carbonate of soda • 270g self-raising flour • 75 g butter • 270 g castor sugar • 3 eggs

Beat the butter and sugar well until the mix is pale and fluffy. Put the dates, water and vanilla in a pan and boil then remove the vanilla pod and discard. Blend to smooth hot paste.

Add the eggs to the butter/sugar mixture, then add the cooled date puree and mix until combined. Sieve the flour and bi-carbonate of soda into the mixture, mix well and pour into a well-greased tin (20cmX 20cm) and bake for around 40-50 minutes at 180 °C, or until a skewer comes out of the pudding clean.

Serve immediately from the oven with tonnes of custard, double cream or you can make a quick salted toffee sauce by putting 100g of muscovado sugar and 200ml of double cream in a pan and melt the sugar gently then add a pinch of sea salt to taste! AMAZING!

CREPES

Remember the golden rule - the first crepe/pancake is always for the chef!

Ingredients (makes about 25 Crepes) - 250g flour • 100g sugar • 6 eggs • Pinch of salt • Vanilla Essence – just a few drops • 75ml Milk

Beat together the eggs and the sugar with the salt and vanilla. Sieve in the flour and beat into a thick paste before adding the milk. Beat into a thinner, smooth batter ready for cooking.

Heat a large frying pan and spray with oil. Ladle out a portion (amounts depend on the size of the pan) Try to get them very thin. You will know they are ready when little bubbles appear in the mixture. Now you're ready to flip!

Is it still in the pan? Is it stuck to the ceiling? Is it on the floor? No? Well done!

I like to serve this with strawberry jam but really anything goes … Lemon juice, chocolate sauce, various ice creams, even peanut butter! Enjoy!

Lemon Tart

Ingredients - 2 lemons - zested and juiced • 6 eggs • 220g caster sugar • 155g double cream

For the pastry - 125g unsalted butter • 2g salt • 65g icing sugar • 2 egg yolks • 220g plain flour

To make the pastry

Using a stand mixer (if possible), mix the butter, salt and sugar together, followed by the egg yolks and then the flour. It should begin to look like bread crumbs. Turn the mixture out onto the work top and work it together lightly with finger tips. Wrap in cling film and chill for 1 hour.

In a large bowl, mix the filling ingredients together (sugar, cream, eggs and lemons), beat well. Roll the pastry out to be as thin as possible. The thickness of a 10 pence piece is the ideal. Line your chosen tart tin or use small individual tins then rest for one hour.

Line with baking beans and bake at 180 °C until the pastry is evenly coloured.
A great tip when blind baking is if you think it's done, it probably isn't! Get a good colour on your pastry as it will help to keep the base crisp for longer!

Sieve the lemony mixture to remove all the zest and any pips that may have dropped in then pour the mixture to the brim of the pastry case and bake at 120 °C for about 35 minutes. If you have a temperature probe use it and cook until the lemon filling reaches 70 °C. If you don't, then bear in mind that the mixture should have a slight wobble in the very centre. Remove and chill over night or in the fridge until needed!

You will not be disappointed with this one!

-RED BERRY-
Knickerbocker
GLORY

$\mathcal{S}$o, there are two ways of doing this recipe, you can go and buy some really great quality ice-cream or sorbet from your local dairy (I use Quorndon ice-cream, www.icecream-sorbet.com) or you can make your own.
It's a little tricky, but here's how.

600g water • 600g sugar • 225g black berries • 225 g raspberries • 125g water • 1 pint Milk • 1 pint double cream • 100g castor sugar • 125g glucose • 6 egg yolks • 1 vanilla pod split and scraped • 200g best quality British strawberries • 200g strawberries • 150g blue berries • 150 g raspberries • 150g raspberries (for the coulis) • 150g icing sugar • can of spray cream • 25g stork • 25g icing sugar • 25g plain flour • 1 egg white

The Sorbet

Firstly make stock syrup. This is a very 'cheffy' word which basically means sugary water. Use equal quantities of water and sugar and simmer in a large pan until the sugar has dissolved.

Meanwhile in a jug, use a stick blender to puree the fresh fruits separately. Sieve out any seeds or fleshy bits.

Put the purees in two separate bowls, add 125g of cold water to each and half of the sugar syrup into the bowls. Whisk well.

Now you have your mixture ready to churn. If you don't have an ice cream machine, put these mixes into shallow trays (like one you would use for lasagne) and place them in the fridge returning every half hour to whisk. This should lighten and fluff up the freezing mixture to "churn it".

This will take a couple of hour's minimum.
Voila! Your sorbet's ready!

Strawberry Ice Cream

Place the milk, cream, glucose and vanilla pod in a large pan. Bring to the boil but be careful - don't boil it over! (It's really messy and quite a pain I have done it far too many times!)

Place the egg yolks and sugar in a bowl and beat well until they look lighter and creamy.

Top tip! Make sure you immediately beat the eggs and sugar together once you put them in the bowl together, otherwise the sugar "burns" the yolks leaving little bits not good.

The milk and cream will come to the boil. When it does, pour it over the egg mixture and beat well to combine. This will form a custard. Return to the pan, turn the heat down and cook slowly until the mixture is thick enough to coat the back of a spoon.

Remove from the heat, place in a clean bowl and chill. Once the mixture is chilled, remove the vanilla pod, puree the strawberries, pass them through a sieve and blend them with the custard mixture. You're ready to churn.

Sadly the method for ice cream isn't quite the same as the method for sorbet. I suggest befriending your local Caterer or restaurant and asking them to churn it for you in return of blinking eyes and sweet smiles. Alternatively, get yourself an ice cream maker!

Tuile

Melt the stork, cool slightly in a bowl. Mix all the ingredients together to make a smooth paste. Chill until cold. Whilst you're waiting for this to chill, take a stencil or template of any shape. I like an obtuse or isosceles triangle but have fun with it and see what you end up with!
On a sheet of baking parchment, use your new template to make triangles all over the parchment with your mixture. Place on a tray and bake at 180 °C until the tuile becomes golden brown – this should be about 5 minutes.
Remove from the oven and experiment with twists and bends! It's fun and doesn't need to be too neat so don't worry!

Coulis

Blend the raspberries with the icing sugar and pass through a sieve to remove any seeds or fleshy bits.
It's up to you how your build your Knickerbocker Glory. I would start with a little coulis at the bottom, add some fresh fruit, then a dollop of ice cream and sorbet, some more fruit… then some more ice cream, coulis, squirty cream, the tuile and perhaps a glace cherry if you wish.

Oh I am salivating! Yummy!

Thomas the Caterer's
VERY SECRET RECIPE
for BROWNIES

Now you're a very privileged person. I have kept this recipe close to my chest for many years! All ovens vary so it may take a few attempts to get this right but when you do, it's fantabulously wonderful and amazing!

Ingredients (makes 10-12 portions you always need extra!) - 300g dark chocolate • 250g unsalted butter • 400g soft light brown sugar • 4 eggs • 190g plain flour

First - Grease and line a square tin – 25cm x 25cm and pre-heat your oven to 170 °C.
Melt the chocolate and butter together, slowly, in a large bowl over a pan of boiling water. Stir in the sugar.
When everything has melted nicely, leave it to cool slightly before adding the eggs one by one - beat well.
Sift the flour into the mixture, fold in and pour into the lined tin. Bake for approximately 30-35 minutes. If you want your brownies especially gooey then take them out after 30 minutes and leave them rest over night! If you prefer a firmer texture, bake for approximately 40 minutes.

(Top Tip - Once you get to know your oven the baking times for this recipe, timings will be irrelevant and you will be able to see if it's cooked to your liking by the cracks in the crust)

Oh I am jealous you're going to make that!

ETON MESS

The perfect summer dessert!

If you're not so keen on the love hearts thing but are a fan of meringue,
then Eton Mess is always a winner! Just follow the recipe for love
heart meringues but break up the meringue and mix with
the whipped cream and berries!

VARIETY OF POTS

These kilner jars are perfect for serving your guests something sweet & delicious at the end of your wedding breakfast. Perhaps a trifle, chocolate mousse or lemony cheescake or this yummy panna cotta.

Vanilla Panna Cotta with Strawberry Compote

Ingredients (serves 6) - 1 litre double cream • 1 vanilla pod - split and scraped • 110g castor sugar • 5 leaves of gelatine • 300g strawberries • 2 tbsp castor sugar • ½ lemon

Boil sugar, cream, vanilla pod and seeds in a large pan. Soak the gelatine leaves in cold water until soft then squeeze excess water out and add to the cream mixture to dissolve. Leave the liquid to cool for 30 minutes then sieve and discard any bits. Pour carefully into 6 separate 250ml kilner jars and chill in the fridge overnight if possible. If not, they should take approximately 6 hours to set.

Around 30 minutes before serving remove from the fridge and leave to reach room temperature - (they eat better this way).

Chop up strawberries into small pieces put into to a bowl with sugar and lemon juice – stir and leave to macerate slightly 20 minutes before serving
Carefully spoon the mixture out into the jars, add a spring of mint and put the lid on the jar!

Voila! A beautifully presented, tasty little dessert.

Thomas decided to be a chef at the tender age of 7. He ate Spaghetti Carbonara for the very first time and knew that food was his chosen path! He has been cooking professionally for over 15 years; and at 30 years old that's officially over half his life in the kitchen!

Aged 15, Thomas got his first apprenticeship in a local restaurant before his passion for food took him across the channel to work in a food lover's paradise, France, for 5 years. He then ventured even further afield to Australia, before falling in love and returning home to base himself in Leicestershire, where he still lives with his family.

He wanted to write this book to express his passion for food and wedding food in particular; to show couples that they don't have to abide by set rules and set menus and that they can in fact create a menu which tells their very own story.

Notes

$\mathcal{N}$otes

Notes

So, you've read the book cover to cover, what did you think?

Did you see anything that inspired you? Was there a recipe that really woke up your taste buds? Maybe we should have a cuppa tea (with some cake perhaps... I like cake) and talk about all your ideas. Perhaps, between us, we could create a yummy menu for your special day. Just give me a call, on 01163 260 529. Or you can email me to organise a meeting on - weddings@thomasthecaterer.co.uk

I can't stress enough, this is just a sneaky preview of just some of the menu options we can create for your wedding. My advice is to be stubborn, be strong and get what you want from your suppliers! You're paying them to get everything exactly how you want it on your Wedding Day!

Lots of Love and Best Wishes from The Kitchen,

Thomas x

A big thank you to everyone who has helped me produce this little book:
Mirlah Thornley - Best Day Ever Stationary, Joanne Withers - Photography, Designer Daisies - Floristry,
Val Mattinson - foreword and wedding planner, Mark Hynds - Design, Katie Westwood - Editor
Photos of Couples by:
Joseph Hall (Thomas and lauren), Eleri Tunstall (Lauren and Ian), Matt Brown (Jessica and Aaron) & Jake Hilder (Emma and James)